W9-CEL-359

ELF
WARFARE

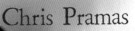

New York

Chris Pramas

This edition published in 2018 by
The Rosen Publishing Group, Inc.
29 East 21st Street
New York, NY 10010

Cataloging-in-Publication Data

Names: Pramas, Chris.
Title: Elf warfare / Chris Pramas.
Description: New York : Rosen YA, 2018. | Series: Creature warfare | Includes glossary and index. | Audience: Grades 7–12.
Identifiers: ISBN 9781508176268 (library bound)
Subjects: LCSH: Elves—Juvenile literature. | War in literature.
Classification: LCC GR549.P73 2018 | DDC 398.21—dc23

Manufactured in China

This edition published by Rosen Publishing by arrangement with Osprey Publishing, an imprint of Bloomsbury Plc.

CONTENTS

CHAPTER ONE:
THE ELVES

This chapter introduces the elf race. It discusses their origins, gods, and magic, and the destructive war that tore the elf kindred apart. It then delves into the organization of the elven military and the arms and equipment it uses.

CHAPTER TWO:
ELF TROOP TYPES

The five elven kindred field a great variety of troops, from core units like archers and spearmen to exotic units like tree runners and moon elf infiltrators. This chapter looks at each in turn, discussing its battlefield role and typical equipment.

CHAPTER THREE:
ELF STRATEGIES AND TACTICS

Elves have been fighting from time immemorial and they have developed many stratagems. This chapter looks at the way that elves win wars. Battlefield tactics, naval tactics, and siege tactics are all looked at in turn.

CHAPTER FOUR:
ELF VICTORIES

Finally Elf Warfare takes a detailed look at five famous victories of elven arms. There is one battle for each of the kindred, showcasing how the various types of elf have been able to win important victories. This chapter also provides some concrete examples of how the myriad of troop types were used in practice.

INTRODUCTION

Elves, like many common creatures in fantasy fiction, have their roots in our myths. They feature in stories that go back a couple of thousand years at least and are present to a greater or lesser degree in all the Germanic mythologies. While some such creatures maintain a fairly cohesive identity over time, elves have changed substantially through the ages. They may have been gods originally but if so, they were demoted from that lofty status. They were still magical beings though and were associated with beauty (though rarely the fun kind). Sometimes they were called demons. Later elves became associated with the fae, and often conflated with various types of faerie. They also shrank alarmingly in this period, becoming tiny creatures in stories and songs. The Victorians gave elves pointed ears and stocking caps, and this led to the form most familiar to modern children: the Christmas elf. All the supernatural threats of previous elves were gone, replaced by tinkers who make toys for Santa Claus. In America elves were reduced even further to makers of sugary cookies.

Elves owe the restoration of their dignity to fantasy fiction. Starting with Lord Dunsany in 1924 in *The King of Elfland's Daughter*, things began to look up for elves. In *The Hobbit* and *The Lord of the Rings*, J.R.R. Tolkien brought them closer to their mythological roots but made them his own as well. Tolkien's elves were ultimately tragic, doomed by their own passions to ages of suffering before abandoning the world all together. With the monumental success of his work, Tolkien's interpretation was widely influential in the field of fantasy and beyond. Now elves – tiny no longer – inhabit hundreds of worlds in fiction and in games.

Elf Warfare is the third series that started with *Orc Warfare* and continued with *Dwarf Warfare*. The goal here is the same: provide a military and cultural analysis of a favorite fantasy race. You'll find concepts and themes that are familiar but some that are different as well. You can enjoy *Elf Warfare* as a work of fantasy in its own right, or a source of ideas for your roleplaying or miniatures game campaigns. The book is broken down into four chapters.

THE ELVES

Since the first sunrise, we have been here. We have lived in the forests and the glens, in the plains and in the mountains, on the sea and under the earth. We are the five kindred. Fire, earth, metal, wood, and water live in us. We are the elements and the seasons. We are nature's beauty and also its wrath. Stand with us and you will prosper. Stand against us and you will be destroyed.

Inscription, Great Temple of the Sun Queen

Elves are a proud and ancient race with a history that stretches back into the mists of time. Their chroniclers claim that elves were there at the world's first sunrise. Dragons might dispute that the elven race is quite that old. Scholars, however, are not rushing off to dragon lairs to ask them their opinion. Suffice to say that elves emerged well before the beginning of recorded history. And they should know – they were the ones who began recording it.

There are five kindred of elves, but they all share common physical characteristics. They are lithe and tall, with an average height of 6 feet. Elves are agile and dexterous, with excellent vision that can pierce the darkness and even better hearing. Their most famous physical characteristic is, of course, their pointed ears. They are a comely race that others often find hauntingly beautiful. Yet elves seem tinged with sadness. Perhaps it is because they live so much longer than other races. Elves live through more heartbreak and tragedy than any human ever could. They can live up to 300 years if their lives are not cut short by violence or calamity. It is a rare elf that lives a full lifespan, however, for the world around them is ugly and brutish. Elves do not always seek war, but too often it finds them.

THE ELVEN KINDRED

At the dawning of the elf race, it was divided into five great kindred. Each was associated with one of the five elements: earth, fire, metal, water, and wood. While each branch had its own strengths and

6

weaknesses, the elves considered themselves to be one people. The Five Kindred settled different lands, but worked together to defeat common enemies. When they were united, the elves were unstoppable.

Alas, the golden age of the Five Kindred could not last. The earth elves got into squabbles with the other kindred. They felt their needs always came last, and their aid, while much desired, was seldom returned in kind. These growing resentments could have been addressed if the other kindred had taken them seriously, but they were busy pursuing their own agendas. Someone did notice, however, and this was to change elf history

forever. The Abyssal Queen, a powerful demon, whispered in the ears of the earth elves. Slowly, she caused the cracks between the elf kindred to become chasms. She turned the earth elves away from their patron god, the Earth Queen, and soon there was war between the kindred.

The Kin-War was long and bitter. The earth elves were outnumbered, but the Abyssal Queen sent demon legions to fight with them. Finally, the loyal kindred defeated the earth elves and drove them deep beneath the surface. Since that time they have been known as the dark elves and they have become an evil and depraved race. The few earth elves who did not fall under the Abyssal Queen's spell became known as the moon elves, for reasons explained later in this chapter.

Today the elves are divided as follows:

Kindred	Common Name	God
Earth Elves (Traitor)	Dark Elves	Abyssal Queen
Earth Elves (Loyal)	Moon Elves	Moon Queen
Fire Elves	High Elves	Sun Queen

Metal Elves	Gold Elves	Sword Queen
Water Elves	Sea Elves	Storm King
Wood Elves	Green Elves	Horned King

Descriptions of gold elves, green elves, high elves, moon elves, and sea elves follow and it is these kindred that are the focus of *Elf Warfare*. Dark elves have taken another path entirely and are thus beyond the scope of this book.

GOLD ELVES

The gold elves are the crafters par excellence of the elven race. They have an affinity with metal that makes their weapons and armor prized by all the civilized peoples, except perhaps the dwarves (who are proud of their own craftsmanship). Originally known as the metal elves, no one calls them that anymore. For one thing, their goldsmithing is unparalleled. For another the sale of their jewelry, rings, and weaponry has made them fabulously wealthy. This has made the gold elves both secretive and cautious.

Once the gold elves lived in great cities like the high elves, but their wealth attracted armies, plunderers, and dragons. Now most remaining gold elf cities are well-hidden in mountain vales laced with glamours to

deceive travelers. A few are entirely underground, but these are more difficult to keep hidden from the dark elves, who never pass up an opportunity to loot a gold elf city. The secretive nature of the gold elf cities makes trade with other elf kindred a slow process, as the first concern of the gold elves is always safety. This has made their creations rarer still, which has only made them more valuable to the outside world.

Not all gold elves want to shut themselves away from the world, however. Rather than retreat to hidden cities, many gold elf clans settled in the lands of other elf kindred. In exchange for security and raw materials, these gold elf clans make weapons and armor for their kin and contribute troops towards the common defense. The clans are most likely to be found in the mighty high elf cities, but they settle among the other kindred as well. The work of expanding and fortifying green elf cavern cities is often undertaken by such clans, for example.

GREEN ELVES

The green elves, also known as the wood elves, are the masters of the great forests. They see themselves as the guardians and the protectors of the woodlands and the creatures that dwell therein. Those who despoil the forests – be they monsters, loggers, or invaders – are guaranteed to face the wrath of the green elves. While they generally keep to themselves and remain in their woodland strongholds, they sometimes send contingents to aid their elven kin. Their archers are particularly prized.

Green elves live in small settlements scattered throughout the forests. Their mages can make trees grow into nearly any shape, and this is how the green elves build their homesteads. Many are tree houses, which provide excellent protection against predators by being high off the ground. All wood elf dwellings are alive and growing. Dead wood and nails are no way to build in green elf lands.

Some green elf bands prefer a nomadic existence. They travel throughout the great forests, making camp and moving on as they please. These bands carry news and sometimes goods from settlement to settlement. Some wood elf cities also exist. Most of them are in natural cave complexes with good water sources that the elves have expanded over time. In times of great peril, many green elves come to these cavern cities to find sanctuary. Their beautiful and spacious galleries can hold many times the typical number of inhabitants, and they have deep stores as well as caverns dedicated to the production of food.

HIGH ELVES

The high elves are the largest and most dynamic of the elf kindred. They burn with an inner fire that drives them to try to master the world. The way they see it, they bring civilization, stability, and enlightenment to a dark and brutish reality. Their enemies would be quick to point out, however, that high elf armies also bring fire, death, and conquest.

The high elves, also known as the fire elves, live in great cities renowned for their strength and beauty. They are centers of learning, both mundane and magical, and also hubs of trade. Other races view these cities with envy and thus they must also be engines of war. So while there are gardens of staggering beauty and a flowering of the arts, there are also barracks and armories scattered throughout every city, and all adult elves must train routinely with spear and bow. There is also a professional army in every city that is always ready to protect its interests.

Of all the elf kindred, it is the high elves who have always been empire builders. They believe that there would be less war if the world was more civilized. Better that they conquer it than savages like the orcs or the endlessly squabbling humans. History has witnessed the spectacular rise and terrible fall of many high elf empires over the millennia. Oftentimes, high elves have ruled over lands encompassing others of their kin. It is not uncommon, for example, for wood elf forests and especially sea elf coastlines to become part of high elf empires. As long as the rulers respect the ways of life of the other kindred, these alliances can be powerful. When the imperious nature of high elves come to the fore that is when the trouble begins.

MOON ELVES

Once the earth elves were one people under the tutelage of their goddess, the Earth Queen. As described earlier in this chapter, a powerful demon known as the Abyssal Queen seduced and corrupted most of the earth elves. After a long and bitter war, these elves – now known as dark elves – were defeated and forced deep beneath the surface. The earth elves who had remained loyal had won a victory of sorts, but it was a hollow one. The Kin-War had decimated their people and the surviving loyalists were few. Worse still, the tragedy had changed the Earth Queen. Now she styled herself the Moon Queen. Once a goddess of birth and stability, she became a goddess of death and madness. Her children, unwilling to abandon her, became the moon elves. They retreated to hidden grottos and since then have maintained a secretive existence.

Even to the other elven kindred, the actions of the moon elves are bizarre. They disappear for decades at a time. They are rumored to practice strange rituals in the pools of their grottos. They often treat other elves with hostility. And yet, on more than one occasion, mysterious bands of moon elves have shown up on the eve of important battles, and fought with valor and sacrifice to ensure elven victory. Then they take their dead and disappear once again.

What the moon elves most desire is to return their goddess to sanity. Their leaders do not agree on how to bring this goal to fruition. Some believe that they must destroy the dark elves and wipe out the stain on their honor. Some think their fallen kin can be redeemed so the earth elves can be one people again. Others think the elven kindred as a whole must unite before the Earth Queen returns to them. The Moon Queen herself provides no answers. Her priests see visions in the grotto pools, but they are cryptic and touched by madness.

SEA ELVES

The sea elves, also known as the water elves, are the great adventurers of their race. They are mariners, explorers, and traders whose wanderlust is legendary. Not for them hiding from the world in forests and cities. Sea elves want to be on the deck of a fast ship with the wind at their back.

The coastline is, of course, where most sea elves dwell when not voyaging. There are pockets of water elves elsewhere, however. Some groups prefer to ply the rivers on great barges. Others settled in swamplands and use flat bottomed boats and skiffs to navigate the waterways. A few brave hidden underground rivers, but they must be forever wary of their dark elf kin.

The towns and smaller settlements of the water elves are perforce somewhat rustic. Many do the less glamorous but just as necessary job of fishing, seafood of course being a staple of their diet. Sea elves, while sometimes characterized as flighty by the high elves, are not bumpkins. There is much travel between their settlements and the far voyagers bring news, stories, and curiosities from all over.

Sea elves themselves are not great city builders, generally favoring to live in towns of a thousand or so elves scattered along their coastlines. Their traders know the value of cities, however, and readily establish themselves when welcomed. It is common, for example, to find sea elf quarters in high elf and even human cities on the coast. Here the trading houses establish themselves and make it their business to become indispensable to their

home cities. In human cities they must walk a fine line, as too much success can make their competitors jealous. Human merchants have driven sea elves out of more than one city when they felt threatened.

ELF ARMIES

The host of all Kallarion readied itself for battle. From all over the empire the eagles had marched and now they united on the blasted plain for the final battle. The dark lord and his numberless minions awaited them. The elves steeled themselves on this day of days. They knew they must win a victory or face annihilation.

From the Chronicles of Kallarion

In ancient times the elves had no formalized military. They lived in scattered clans that were largely self-sufficient. In times of trouble, the able-bodied folk would gather under the chief and form what was called a clan-troop. These could vary in size between a dozen warriors to several hundred, depending on the size of the clan. Elven clans would sometimes join together to fight a common foe but these were temporary arrangements. Even today there are elves who live and fight in this fashion, most commonly wood elves and moon elves.

It was the high elves, with their dreams of empire, who advanced the military arts over the millennia. They created standing armies in their cities and organized them according to a common pattern, which then spread to other elven kindred. The elvish name for these armies translates to "glorious eagles of war and victory" but only the stuffiest academic text uses that terminology now. To soldiers, citizens, friends, and enemies, elven armies are known as eagles. Their structure varies somewhat by time and place, but typically an elf army is organized as follows:

- An eagle consists of at least two wings and is commanded by a general.
- A wing consists of three to ten talons and is commanded by a major.
- A talon consists of three to five troops and is commanded by a captain.
- A troop consists of twelve to twenty soldiers and is commanded by a sergeant.

As elves are small in number compared to their enemies, all adult elves who are able must spend time in military training. Typically, this is a three year period but in some places it is up to ten years. In those years the elves' primary job is that of a soldier, with training in melee and missile combat, maneuvering in formation, and battle tactics. Once this period of active service ends, they can go back to their civilian lives if they so choose. They remain on the rolls of their talon, however, and each summer they muster again for a few weeks to refresh their skills and meet and interact with the younger recruits. In this way the elves can call up nearly their entire adult population in times of war. Most crises are not so dire, so younger elves are called up first by year. When the aged veterans are called to serve, the situation must be truly desperate.

THE PROFESSIONALS

Some elves choose not to return to civilian life and become full time, professional soldiers. In times of peace their numbers are relatively small. Long service soldiers typically become sergeants or officers, though some become part of elite formations like the Star Knights. Major elven cities are home to military academies that train officers in strategy and tactics. Promising soldiers from all over vie to get into these prestigious schools. Military academies are typically a ten year commitment that mix classes with field training. Candidates graduate not just with a sound basis in theory but also with years of hands-on practice.

The wood elves and others without access to military academies use a mentorship system to train officers. Candidates are assigned as assistants to serving officers and learn on the job. The training is perforce less standardized but still can produce outstanding leaders. Typically under this system there is one mentor and one mentee. It's been found that this gives the best results, as the officer can concentrate on teaching the one candidate. If a war drags on, however, an officer may have to take on up to half-dozen mentees at once so the fallen can be replaced quickly.

ELF ARMOR AND WEAPONS

Elves are a long-lived race and their craftsmanship reflects this. While they can, when the need is acute, make things quickly, they prefer to take their time and make their crafts both functional and beautiful. This applies to weapons and armor just as much as it does to clothing and jewelry. Form matters as much as function, and sometimes even more so. A sword etched with a pattern of blooming flowers is cherished more than an unadorned blade, even if the latter cuts deeper.

As elves are generally tall and lithe, they prefer weapons that are lighter and quicker than many of their foes. They know that enemies like orcs and ogres are stronger than they are, so they rely on speed and skill to beat such opponents. Their weapons are designed to maximize the elves' natural gifts of agility and quickness. Similarly, armor is designed for the most protection with the least weight. None of this would be possible without the skill of elven smiths. They have spent millennia perfecting techniques that allow them to forge steel that is light but incredibly strong. This work is so beyond the skill of human smiths that they think the elves are working with a special metal not found in human lands. Stories of "faerie steel" are common, and elven smiths do little to dispel them. Their skills and techniques are the real treasure, so they'd rather have humans chasing a mythical metal than trying to learn their secrets.

Elves use a broad range of armor. Green elves, moon elves, and other light troops favor leather armor, as speed and stealth are integral to their tactics. Sea elves prefer it too, as heavier armor is a detriment when fighting on the water. High elves and other melee troops favor chainmail, as it provides a balance of weight and protection. Gold elves and certain elite units use plate armor, which offers unrivaled protection though at a high cost.

The most common melee weapons are spears and long swords. Spears are usually between 6 and 9 feet in length, though some units have been known to use weapons up to 12 feet long when facing cavalry heavy armies. Light troops favor short swords and sometimes hatchets. Battle axes are sometimes used but are much less common. Perhaps it is their long association with dwarves that puts elves off. Two-handed weapons like glaives and great swords are rarest of all, usually only used by elite formations like foot knights.

The weapon most associated with elves is, of course, the bow. Elf bowyers are just as skilled as the smiths and the elven longbow is truly a work of art. When used by properly trained archers (a process that takes many years), they shoot farther and hit harder than human or orc bows. The longbow is by far the most prevalent type of bow in use in elf eagles, but light cavalry and certain units like companions use the composite short bow instead. This cannot shoot as far as the longbow, but it handles more easily and still packs a punch.

The fletchers provide a variety of arrows for elf archers. The most common types are leaf arrows and branch arrows. Leaf arrows take their name from the broad shape of their arrowheads, and they are used in hunting and against lightly armored opponents in times of war. Even a glancing hit from a leaf arrow can cause a long cut that bleeds heavily. When facing more heavily armored foes, archers turn to branch arrows. These arrows have narrow heads with either a spike or a chisel point. The skill of elf smiths is once again on display with these arrowheads, as their points are hard enough to penetrate most armor. The spike variant works best against chainmail while the chisel variant is designed to punch through plate armor. Elf archers usually carry a mix of all these types of arrow.

Units of archers describe themselves as trunks from which sprout branch and leaf. Some elf units also use arrows for signaling. This is done using arrows that make whistling sounds. Different pitches indicate different orders. Even foes who understand that the elves are signaling each other don't have the ear for music that allows the elves to tell the subtle differences in pitch that indicate various commands.

ELF MAGIC

Elves are masters of magic. They have few rivals in this arena, for they have been studying magic for eons. That said, the path of the wizard is long and dangerous, and the number of powerful elf wizards is small. While the generals wish it were otherwise, it's a rarity that a wizard actually takes the field with an elven eagle. The nature of elven spellcraft is also a disappointment to war makers who want flashy and destructive magic on call. Wizards mostly use ritual magic, which can indeed be quite destructive, but rituals can take days and even months to complete. This is not helpful when a battle is going to be fought today. Ritual magic can have a powerful effect on military campaigns in the long term though. Elf wizards can summon up storms to lash enemy armies or bog them down in mud given the right circumstances. If the elves besiege a fortress or city, wizards could use earth magic to shake down its walls given time.

Elven magic is based on the five elements and the four seasons. It is a common misconception that each kindred can only use magic from its associated element. Many human scholars believe, for example, that high elves can only use fire magic and green elves can only use wood magic. In truth elves of one kindred have an aptitude for their element, but can learn magic of any element. Indeed, they must because elf magic is all about the complicated interplay of the elements and also the season. Certain rituals work better when cast in the appropriate season. A ritual to increase the fertility of land works best in spring, for example.

Elf magic comes into play in wartime most commonly in two ways: defensive enchantments and magic items. Defensive enchantments are effective because the rituals can be cast in times of peace, when time is an abundance resource. All but the youngest of elf cities, for example, have had their walls and towers fortified by earth magic. This makes them much more difficult to breach during a siege. Similarly, green elf forests are protected by a variety of enchantments to confuse and mislead invaders. Once enemies get inside an elven forest, they find it difficult to navigate and are easily lured into traps and ambushes. Elven ships are fast and durable because their planks are enchanted with water magic.

Magic items is a broad category that covers a variety of portable artifacts. Those most commonly seen on the battlefield are weapons and armor, and gold elves are the undisputed masters of this type of magic. Wizards of other kindred can and do use metal magic, but the gold elves' natural aptitude and millennia of practice make them the most skilled forgers and enchanters of magic weapons and armor. They can make weapons that can puncture plate armor with ease, and shields that can stand up to the mightiest blows. Some weapons burn with an inner heat or crackle with electricity. Others can freeze an opponent's limbs. Arrows are the most common magic item seen in elven eagles, as several can be enchanted at once. Most are simply better at penetrating armor. Some carry other effects, like bursting into flame on contact or causing wounds that won't heal naturally.

For themselves wizards make magic wands or staves. These they use for self-defense and to make direct attacks on the battlefield. Wands and staves take years to enchant and each has a limited number of magic effects. Some are always active. These are typically defensive, like an enchantment to protect the wizard from arrows and other missiles. Others can be used a certain number of times per day. Depending on the spell, its use may be limited to daylight or nighttime. The most destructive effects (lightning bolts, gouts of fire, etc.) can only be used once in a battle. A wizard with a powerful wand or stave can change the course of a battle, but the number of such wizards is small.

ELF TROOP TYPES

Elven armies are quite varied, as each of the kindred fights in its own way. Some troop types are common among all the kindred and others are unique to one or two. This chapter breaks down the various elements of elven eagles and looks at each in detail. Enemy generals who think that every elven army is the same are in for a surprise.

ARCHERS

We outnumbered the elf army but many of our infantry units were made up of ill-trained conscripts with little in the way of training or armor. I told the general a frontal attack was suicide. He called me a coward and led the charge in person. It is a mercy he was killed in the first volley. He never had to see the army break and run or the piles of arrow riddled corpses.

Nasreen, Human Commander of Horse

Archers are the heart of the elven military tradition. Simply put, there are no better units of missile troops than elven archers. Some say that elves are just natural marksmen, but there is more to it than that. It is true that elves are dexterous by nature, with excellent hand/eye coordination. Equipment and training are just as important, however. Elves long ago mastered the arts of bowyer and fletcher. The elven longbow is a powerful weapon but all but useless to those without proper training. Thus elves of all kindred start at a young age and that training never ceases. Even the oldest elves still come out to archery butts a couple of times a week. Younger elves shoot every day. Clans, towns, and cities have regular competitions to encourage the pursuit of marksmanship.

In times of war up to half of an elven force may consist of archers. In some case the percentage is even higher. They are deployed and used in different ways, depending on the situation and the kindred involved. Green elf archers usually fight as skirmishers, which makes sense for forest terrain. High and gold elf archers can use skirmish tactics, but also form up into large units that can unleash devastating volleys. Sea elf training focuses on naval combat. Their role is to sweep enemy decks of their crew with accurate fire. Due to their small numbers, moon elves most often take on the role of snipers. They target leaders and standard bearers, with the aim of undermining the enemy's morale.

Archers are usually lightly armored, with leather jerkins or perhaps chainmail shirts. They carry short swords or dirks for close defense, and while quite adept with those weapons they can't stand for long against enemy shock troops. An elven archer generally goes into battle with at least 40 arrows and keeping them supplied is an important part of any battle plan. Their rate of fire is such that they can loose all their arrows in a matter of minutes. Support troops must be ready with fresh arrows or the archers will become a spent force in short order.

SPEARMEN

The wagons with the wounded need time to get to safety. We plant our spears here and we will not be moved!

Melidel, Elf Captain

Spearman are the most common melee troops in elven armies. They fight in close formation, creating a thicket of spear points that can repel both cavalry and infantry formations. Most such units wear chainmail and carry shields they can interlock for increased defense. They carry short swords as secondary weapons, which can be quite handy when enemies get beyond units' spear points.

High elves deploy their spearmen in large phalanxes that are difficult to shift. These units are up to ten ranks deep, and when they push forward they are hard to resist. Gold elves developed an even heavier type of unit that eschewed shields so they could wield longer and longer spears. These days such troops wear plate armor for protection and use both hands to handle pikes that are up to 16 feet long.

Green elves, though identified strongly with hit and run missile tactics, do maintain units of spearmen, though they use them differently than their kindred. They can and do form shield walls, especially when they want to block choke points in the forest. Green elf spearmen can form up and tear down a shield wall in a matter of seconds, though they are typically only three or four ranks deep. They are not designed to get into long slogging matches with enemy troops, however. They are meant to have short, sharp engagements while other green elf troops perform flanking maneuvers and bring more archers to bear.

SWORDSMEN

Arrows killed my horse so I found myself on foot once again. I had just gathered a few of my men when elf swordsmen slammed into our flank. I thought I was a fair bladesman but they went through us in seconds and I was left for dead.

Thestor, Human Mercenary Sergeant

While archers and spearmen are the dominant types of elven infantry, units of swordsmen also appear in the order of battle. They provide eagles with a solid medium infantry that is able to attack or defend as tactics require. Swordsmen typically wear full chainmail armor and carry large shields. They wield long swords designed for slashing and thrusting as the situation merits. These "sword and board" troops can hold their own against most enemy infantry once they are formed up. Typically, units of swordsmen are deployed behind spearmen and are used to shore up the battle line or counter-attack once the enemy has lost its impetus. They are skilled fighters, many of whom have spent decades learning the finer points of bladework.

High elves field swordsmen most frequently and often use them as garrison troops. Gold elves prefer heavy infantry but do field swordsmen to fill out their ranks. Green, moon, and sea elves prefer their swordsmen to be less encumbered, so they wear chain shirts only and carry smaller shields. This makes them more mobile, which suits the fighting style of those kindred better.

FOOT KNIGHTS

Two of the knights with glaives used their weapons to trip the rampaging troll. It only fell to its knees but that was enough. My two-handed sword crunched into its neck. The troll looked at me stupidly, as its blood gushed all over. Then it fell on its face and expired.

Selwyn, Knight of the Chalice

The heaviest infantry in an elven eagle are the foot knights. They are elite formations made up of highly trained warriors in full plate armor and wielding two-handed weapons such as halberds, glaives, and great swords. Gold elves and high elves maintain knightly orders to recruit and train these feared shock troops. The most famous of these orders are the gold elves' Knights of the Chalice and the high elves' Knights of the Phoenix. Entry into these orders is based on merit only. Family bloodlines are not considered. Candidates must be experienced warriors with proven skill, strength, and endurance. Foot knights must face the toughest opponents on the battlefield and they must be ready for them.

The foot knights have a friendly rivalry with their mounted brethren such as the Star Knights and Griffon Knights. They consider the mounted knights to be glory hounds who want to win the battle with one charge. The foot knights pride themselves on their ability to get into extended slogging matches with the fiercest enemies and come out victorious. When trolls or orc Ironbacks are rampaging though the battleline, it is the foot knights who are called upon to stop them. Only they have the armor, weapons, and expertise to deal with enemy shock troops.

As they are elite troops and expensive to maintain, the number of foot knights is never large. A typical elven eagle might have one unit of foot knights and they must be used judiciously. They often act as a bodyguard to the general until the moment of decision arrives. Then they are committed where the danger is the greatest. Some generals like to lead them personally into the fray. While this is an honor, most foot knights prefer it if the general stays backs and concentrates on commanding the eagle. Only the rarest of generals has the skill to keep up with the foot knights and they'd rather focus on defeating the enemy than protecting a leader who is not well-versed in their fighting style.

COMPANIONS

We tore into the elf line, hammering down on their shields and driving them back. We pushed them and pushed them but suddenly the line firmed up and orcs were falling all around me. I turned around to wave the boys forward but there was no one left behind me. Sneaky elves with puny bows had shot them all down.

Torgar, Orc Warchief

Companions are specially trained and equipped archers pioneered by gold elves but sometimes used by other kindred as well. Unlike regular archers, they use composite short bows instead of longbows and wear full chainmail. Their role on the battlefield is to provide close support to melee troops. Companions must be able to fight in formation or in skirmish order, shoot accurately while the melee swirls close by, and know when to engage and when to break off. This requires discipline, good judgment, and a great deal of training.

A unit of companions forms immediately behind a melee unit such as spearmen, swordsmen, or foot knights. Typically, these two units train together, as they must fight in unison on the battlefield. Companions let other archer units shoot at long range and begin the reduction of enemy numbers. As enemy melee troops approach, companions began to shoot volleys of arrows. When this is no longer practical, they break into a skirmish formation and take up position on either side of the unit they have been paired with. In the ensuing melee, they move around the flanks of the enemy unit if possible and shoot at it at point blank range. Here the power of the composite bow comes into its own and companions shoot the enemy down at ranges closer than any other archers would dare. If they cannot flank the enemy, they shoot over the heads of their allies into the rear ranks of the enemy.

Companions carry short swords and when necessary, they can get stuck into a melee but this is a last resort. They provide better support with their bows. They are particularly lethal when enemy units break and run. Companions can continue shooting into the exposed backs of their foes long after the elf melee troops have stopped their pursuit.

SCOUTS

The scouts report that the dwarves have split their war host in two. One part is heading for the bridge and the other the ford upstream. This is the chance we've been waiting for. We can concentrate our wings on one of these forces

Scouts are the eyes and ears of an elven army. They are recruited out of the archers and each one is an expert shot and tracker. They are also masters of stealth and camouflage, and can move unnoticed in most terrain. Their primary job is not to attack, but to monitor enemy movements and make sure elven commanders have a clear picture of what is happening on the battlefield. They communicate this information through coded signals or runners. The signals sound like bird calls to the untrained ear but scouts can transit sophisticated information using this method. For particularly important messages, they will send a runner back to headquarters. Since scouts usually operate in troops of a dozen or so, the number of runners available is perforce limited.

Scouts can and do fight when necessary. Most frequently, they clash with their opposite number. If they detect enemy scouts in the field, they attempt to mislead them or ambush them if this proves impossible. Denying the enemy's leadership information is an important task. Scouts sometimes attack isolated enemy units to sow confusion in their ranks as well.

Elven scouts carry bows and short swords, and sometimes hatchets as well. The latter are useful for woodcraft and can also be used in hand to hand combat. A few scouts wear leather armor but most wear no armor at all. They need to be able to move quickly and silently and most don't want the weight of even leather armor when they are on a mission. This is another reason the quick strike from ambush is their preferred tactic. They are not cut out for a drawn out fight. If things go wrong, scouts melt back into cover and make their way back to elven lines.

TREE RUNNERS

That forest was a death trap. Dealing with the elves shooting at you from behind every tree was bad enough, but arrows also rained down on us from archers up in the trees! Tricky buggers never came down to fight us with honor, just ran through the branches and pelted us with missiles. I've never seen so many head wounds in all my years of campaigning.

Valan, Human Soldier

Among the green elves there is a cadre of skirmishers who specialize in three-dimensional warfare. While all wood elves are skilled climbers, the tree runners are capable of amazing acrobatic feats. They can move quickly in the treetops, jumping from bough to bough. In the dense forests of the great green elf homelands, they can make lengthy journeys without their feet touching the ground.

Due to their stealth and agility, tree runners excel at ambush tactics. Most commonly, they will position themselves above and behind an enemy unit and then unleash volleys of arrows upon them. In dark and tangled forests, it is not immediately obvious where the attack is coming from and this only adds to the confusion. Some tree runners like to get right over a unit and throw javelins or drop rocks on enemies instead. Caches of these weapons, as well as extra arrows, are prepared beforehand and hidden up in trees in likely avenues of approach.

Tree runners with time to plan also prepare traps in their chosen ambush sites. They may seed the ground with caltrops to hamper enemy movement. They may use rope to suspend heavy stones or dead wood from tree branches, ready to drop these on unsuspecting enemies. They've even been known to locate beehives before an engagement, so they can be thrown into enemy units. The hive itself does little damage but the angry bees that burst forth can create chaos in disordered enemy units. If faced with a weight of return missile fire, tree runners disappear into the treetops and redeploy somewhere else. They are a devilish nuisance to enemy commanders, who have been known to resort to lighting fires to smoke them out of the trees. Starting a fire in the middle of the forest your army occupies is, of course, not always the best idea…

MOON ELF INFILTRATORS

The general's tent was like an abattoir. So much blood. He and all his bodyguards were dead. And though there were troops not ten yards away, no one had heard a thing. No clang of weapons. No death screams. Nothing.

Stoddard, Priest of the Emerald Order

Moon elves are the smallest kindred by far. They do maintain units of traditional elven troop types, but they have had to learn to make war in other ways. The infiltrators typify this style of fighting. They are small teams of two to twelve soldiers who specialize in irregular warfare. They use ambush and hit and run tactics to cause confusion behind enemy lines. They are masters of night fighting, using stealth techniques and their elven vision to turn darkness into a time of terror for the foe. They have also been known to perform decapitation strikes against enemy leadership. Sometimes they will conceal themselves on a battlefield the night before an expected battle, only revealing themselves when they

have a chance to kill important leaders like generals or spell casters. This has changed the course of several important battles. However, the moon elves make their own plans and do not share them with their allies, which sometimes leads to tension. Their operations sometimes wrong foot their allies, but the moon elves as always pursue their own goals.

Since infiltrators rely on stealth, they are generally lightly armed and armored. In most engagements they wear leather armor and carry compact weapons like short swords, hand crossbows, daggers, and short bows. Some have mastered unusual weapons like whips and crescent staves. The latter are short staves with a blade in the shape of a crescent moon. An infiltrator typically fights with one in each hand, but they can also be snapped together to form a longer weapon with a blade on each end. This is done when the fighting gets hot and survival becomes more important than stealth.

MARINES

The seaward wall was all but undefended in the siege. It was impossible to land troops there, or so we thought. Damn sea elves swam over the reef and then scaled the walls while we slept. We woke the next morning to find the gates of the city open and elf marines in the towers drinking our booze.

Randulick, Guard of the Tragano Garrison

Elven warships have contingents of specially trained soldiers, the vast majority of whom are sea elves. The job of the marines is not to sail the ship (that's what the sailors do) but to fight. They specialize in boarding actions, and are well-versed in offensive and defensive tactics in ship combat. When their ship closes with an enemy vessel, it is the marines who swarm over the gap to seize it.

At sea the marines do not usually fight in formation. Boarding actions are much more chaotic affairs, so they fight in loose groups at best. As both hands are often needed for balance, few marines use shields. Heavy armor is also not prudent when at sea, so leather jacks and chain shirts are about the only armor used and even they are rare. Armament is very much an individual choice to a marine. They are generally armed with some combination of cutlasses, rapiers, hand axes, maces, and boarding pikes. About a quarter of the marines also have bows. They tend to stay on their own vessel and provide support for the attackers, or defend the ship if it is being boarded. Full units of sea elf archers are also sometimes assigned to a ship, particularly if a naval battle is expected.

While marines' primary role is shipboard combat, they do sometimes fight on land. They may be landed to attack a fort or a town. In dire circumstances, the navy sends a unit of marines to reinforce the eagles. The marines don't particularly care for this kind of combat. Their training is not in formed units and shoulder to shoulder fighting. Still, the marines have their uses in a land battle. They can be fielded as light infantry, dealing with enemy skirmishers, raiding baggage trains, and the like. They have, on occasion, served as garrison troops, but generals prefer other troops for such duty. Leaving marines in the proximity of so many taverns is an invitation to indiscipline.

BEAST HANDLERS

The elves are always on about how much more civilized they are than us. Tell that to my soldiers who were ripped apart by wild dogs!

Sergeant Minyas, The Azure Company

In ancient times elves of all the kindred used animals in battle. Today it is primarily the green elves who carry on that tradition. Every community includes expert beast handlers. Some of them take care of horses and others domestic animals, but a specialized core of handlers train animals for war.

The favored animal for this is the so-called elven woodhound, a tough breed of dog that excels at hunting and takes easily to battle training. Woodhounds are fast and pugnacious. They can bowl over an infantryman or drag lightly armored cavalry from the back of their mounts. Some woodhounds are even fitted with hardened leather armor for protection, which is often spiked to make them difficult to grapple with. Other animals sometimes trained by beast handlers include the kellinor (a big cat similar to a puma), hawks, and even bears on occasion. Various other birds are also used for communication purposes. The moon elves don't use animals to fight, but they do use owls to carry messages between their communities.

In times of war the beast handlers choose their animals and guide them carefully to the field of battle. The handlers themselves wear little armor so they can keep up a good pace. They are typically armed with a bundle of javelins and a short sword. They fight if necessary but their job is to direct the animals and to control them as much as possible. They are also trained in husbandry and can treat their animals' wounds after the battle is over.

LIGHT CAVALRY

Dwarf ballistas are deploying on the right flank. We must ride down their crews before they get those machines set up and shooting. Follow me, sabers at the ready. Speed of horse!

Telewyn, Elf Captain

Elven armies maintain various units of light cavalry for reconnaissance, communication, and pursuit. The green elves have their Forest Riders, the high elves their Border Rangers, the sea elves their Coast Watchers, the gold elves their Steel Wardens, and the moon elves their Night Stalkers. All of these units share common equipment and tactics. Light cavalry are usually armed with composite short bows and curved sabers ideal for passing slashing attacks. Some also carry spears or javelins. They wear either leather armor or chainmail.

The main responsibility of the light cavalry is finding the enemy and keeping track of their movements. On their swift elven steeds, they are difficult to catch and this lets them range far afield when scouting. Their speed makes it possible to provide timely intelligence to commanders on enemy dispositions. They also try to detect and neutralize enemy scouts.

Once battle is joined, light cavalry can take on many different roles. All are skilled horse archers, so they can speedily bring enemy units under fire and then ride away when threatened. Their sabers come out when dealing with enemy light troops, be they infantry or cavalry. When enemy units break and flee, the light cavalry ride them down swiftly.

HEAVY CAVALRY

The charge of the Griffon Knights was the most beautiful spectacle I have ever seen in a lifetime of campaigning. The glittering golden armor, the snapping pennants, the thundering horses — it was magnificent. I was so caught up in the moment I almost took a lance to the face.

Chellain, Paladin of the Pierced Heart

The heavy cavalry is the armored fist of an elven army. They are tall, strong elves on powerful steeds. High elves and gold elves are the kindred that make most use of heavy cavalry and it is their Star Knights and Griffon Knights respectively that are the most famous.

Heavy cavalry wear full plate armor and large shields, and are armed with lances, long swords, and maces, as befits their melee combat role. Their war horses too are armored with barding, which slows them down some but provides important protection. The cost in time and gold to train and outfit such troops is tremendous, so they are not committed to battle lightly. They simply cannot be replaced quickly so elven generals are always careful when deploying heavy cavalry.

Typically, the heavy cavalry are kept in reserve and committed when the battle swings in the balance. Their job is at once simple and difficult: break the enemy's main line of resistance. Most commonly this means crushing blocks of heavy infantry, though sometimes they face cavalry or even large creatures like ogres. Their most potent weapon is the charge. A line of elven knights thundering forward with lances leveled is nigh unstoppable. If they can impact and break the enemy with such a charge, it can end a battle. If the heavy cavalry gets bogged down in a lengthy melee, that's when it becomes vulnerable.

DRAGOONS

The day we captured General D'Bruzza was truly glorious. He had ridden ahead of his army with a light escort to the frontier fort he planned to use as his headquarters in the coming campaign. We left the front gate open and he rode right in. Imagine his surprise to find the fort already occupied by several hundred dragoons!

Neniel, Elf Dragoon

Dragoons are mounted infantry troops. Unlike cavalry, they are not trained or equipped to fight on horseback. Rather they use horses for transport but dismount to fight. Dragoons were pioneered, strangely enough, by the sea elves. When they raided from their ships, sea elf sailors and marines would seize all the horses and mules they could find and use them to cover ground more quickly. Infantrymen grumbled that this was because seamen couldn't handle a day of real marching, but military leaders realized the idea had merit. Soon other kindred were experimenting with mounted infantry and now they are a regular feature of gold elf and high elf armies. Moon elves also took the concept. It allows them to deploy speedily, but then dismount and use the stealth tactics they are famous for. The name dragoon is derived from a now famous incident in which a high elf knight asked a sea elf on a stolen mule what he was supposed to be. "A dragon of the sea!" the soldier replied proudly. The sea elf's low brow accent confused the knight, who asked, "What on earth is a dragoon?" The story spread and the name stuck.

Most dragoons are armed and equipped as swordsmen, spearmen, or companions. About a quarter of their number are archers. They are used when it's imperative to get infantry to a strategic point as soon as possible. They frequently join light and heavy cavalry to form flying columns that can confound the enemy with lightning attacks. They are capable of fighting on horseback when necessary but they are not true cavalry and only a foolish commander uses them that way. If dragoons have a downside it's that some of their soldiers must remain with the horses once the unit dismounts. Usually one out of every five dragoons is on this duty, meaning the unit is almost never able to use its full strength when fighting on foot. Some units bring grooms with them to watch the horses, but such non-combatants are vulnerable in the situations dragoons often find themselves in.

LIGHT CHARIOTS

I guided my wolf over the hill and there before me I saw elf chariots streaming out of the forest. Elves in chariots – was I really seeing this? Did I drink too much fire water last night? Did the Smite-Father hit me upside the head?

Marguz, Goblin Wolf Archer

Chariots are a weapon of war that featured heavily in the early annals of the elves but are rarely used today. The only place chariots are found in any numbers is among the green elves, but even they mostly use them for sporting competitions. In the great glades sometimes found in wood elf lands, there are traditionally chariot races to celebrate the first day of summer. Generally, the green elves try to use the claustrophobic nature of the forests to their advantage in times of war, which usually rules out the large areas of flat terrain best for chariots. There are times, however, when chariots still race into the fray.

Battles do happen from time to time in the aforementioned glades. In the rare cases when green elf armies sally forth from their homelands, they sometimes march into terrain quite suitable for chariots. In these cases the light chariots are crewed and used in battle. Their primary role is that of mobile shooting platform. Elven chariots are designed for two crew, one driver and one archer. Units of light chariots race about the field, sending arrows into the enemy and then moving away. Sometimes the chariots are also used to quickly deploy units of foot archers. Each chariot picks up one archer from the foot troops and carries them quickly to where they are needed. The chariot archers cover them with shots while the foot archers form up. Then they speed away to carry on with their own activities. If needed, they can recover the foot archers and bring them back to the main battle line.

WAR MACHINES

Elf war machines are functional enough, certainly better than those orc pieces of junk. And of course they are pretty to look at because that's what elves like to waste their time on. Do they have the precision engineering of dwarf war machines though? I think not!

Rorik, Dwarf Engineer

The gold elves were the first of the kindred to develop war machines. From there they spread to the high elves, who needed such weapons to fulfil their dreams of conquest, and later the sea elves, who used them to arm their ships. The moon elves eschew war machines, perhaps in part because their traitorous dark elf brethren have embraced them. Green elves use war machines on occasion but they do not fit well with their style of warfare.

Elf eagles take war machines to field battles infrequently. They are slow to transport and set up, and elf generals prefer a quicker tempo of warfare. They are most often used to defend elf fortifications or to attack those of the enemy. Gold elf cities are bristling with war machines, and high elf cities are not far behind.

The most common elf war machine is the ballista, which is essentially an enormous crossbow that shoots spears across the battlefield. The spearheads can be covered in pitch, converting them into flaming weapons at a cost of some loss of accuracy. Sea elf crews do this routinely in their naval battles, as ships are large targets and fire a deadly weapon.

The elf ballista has two variants: heavy and light. The heavy ballista is large enough that it is essentially immobile. It is used as a siege weapon or mounted on ships and needs a crew of five or six. Those eagles that do bring war machines to the field favor the light ballista. They only require a crew of two or three elves to operate and have proved useful when facing monstrous foes like trolls. The elven gift of marksmanship is apparent in all the ballista crews. The dwarves may have ballistas that shoot faster, but elf ballistas are incredibly accurate.

In sieges elf engineers build trebuchets, large stone throwers that use a counter-weight mechanism. These well-designed machines can hurl rocks that weigh hundreds of pounds at walls and towers and inflict punishing damage. Trebuchets are large, heavy, and immobile, and they require large crews to operate efficiently.

MONSTROUS ALLIES

It was a bright and cloudless day but suddenly we were in shadow. I looked up and there was a griffon dropping from the sky! It crushed a half dozen men and then tore into the survivors with claws and beak. We ran and the neighboring units followed us. No amount of gold was enough to face that thing.

Bergliot, Human Mercenary

In ancient times the elves made pacts with some of the more intelligent monstrous races. Even in those days it was uncommon to see creatures like griffons, giant eagles, and dragons fighting alongside elven armies but they played an important role in several famous battles and these deeds are still frequent topics of poetry and song. These days monstrous allies on the battlefield are a rare sight indeed for two reasons. First, the numbers of such creatures has dwindled over the millennia. Second, there are few living wizards who are skilled in this sort of a magic. Summoning a monstrous ally requires the use of a magical ritual keyed to the ancient pacts. An elven wizard must both know the appropriate ritual and know the name and location of a suitable creature. This information can be hard to come by. Still, it does happen from time to time that a mighty griffon or fire-spewing dragon arrives on the battlefield to aid the elf kindred. Such creatures cannot be controlled, so commanders must be agile when a monstrous ally appears and take best advantage of the havoc they wreak.

VELLADOR ALLIES

Our ancestors swore mighty oaths to the elven kingdoms. We had to cross the mountains and fight our way through two armies but we are here. The Vellador do not take their oaths lightly.

Caralorgas, General of the Seven Cities

In ancient times the elves made alliances with human tribes that had proved themselves loyal and trustworthy. In exchange for aiding the elves in the battle, these tribes received gifts. At first these were simply implements of war; armor and weapons finer than anything the humans could make for themselves. Over time the elves passed on something even more valuable: knowledge. They taught the humans engineering, philosophy, and even some magic. These tribes went on to found their own cities and countries that were, while heavily influenced by elven thought, still of human character. The elves dubbed these humans Vellador, which translates roughly to "our civilized cousins." The Vellador often refer to themselves as "high men" and consider themselves superior to other humans (see Cullador Allies following).

The Vellador have long been tied to the elves by treaties of friendship and alliance. They can be relied upon to provide troops to the elves in times of need and receive elven help in return. They are most commonly allied with high elves, but alliances with sea elves and gold elves are known. Since the Vellador have benefited from centuries of elven military training, their armies tend to look quite similar to those of the high elves. They have equivalents to most elven troop types and in most situations will send a well-balanced army of infantry and cavalry to their allies.

The elves trust the Vellador and this manifests itself in some important ways. First, Vellador troops are allowed inside elven cities and fortresses, which is a rare honor. Second, elven generals value these troops and do not squander their lives casually. They want the Vellador to come the next time their aid is needed.

CULLADOR ALLIES

The orcs charged our line three times that day. Some sea elf swordsmen stood with us but the rest of the elves were engaged elsewhere. I lost half my command in one afternoon but there was no way we were going to let the orcs break through. I wanted the elves to see what so-called barbarians could do.

Hegener, Human Commander

The Vellador are valued but their numbers are relatively small. There are many more human tribes, cities, and nations out there who never received elven tutelage. They are called the Cullador, which roughly translates to "our barbarian cousins." Many Cullador cities are quite advanced and they resent what they see as elvish snobbery. They also reject the implication that they are "low men" compared to the Vellador. In any case, the elves still trade and form alliances with nearby human settlements, as they often have common enemies.

For elf generals Cullador troops provide the numbers that their armies lack. Elves are skilled soldiers but their numbers are not great. Cullador troops can help redress the balance when fighting armies like the orcs. For this reason the allied troops the elves value most are simple foot soldiers. Blocks of spearmen, swordsmen, and crossbowmen are useful for reinforcing the battle line. It would be unfair to say that elven generals do not value Cullador lives, but it must be said that their casualties are a secondary concern.

Cullador troops are often used to guard lines of march and communication, but unlike the Vellador they are not allowed into elven cities and fortresses. Cities have fallen at the hands of traitors before, and elf leaders do not want to take any chances. It is possible for Cullador to be elevated to the status of Vellador through loyal service, but this is rare.

ELF STRATEGIES AND TACTICS

Elves have been waging war for countless millennia. The high elves sought it out, sending armies of conquest hither and yon. The dark elves tore their race apart in the Kin-War. All the kindred have had to deal with invaders and tyrants set on their destruction. As the elves are inveterate writers and record keepers, there is a body of military knowledge that stretches back to antiquity. The military academies delve deep into this lore when teaching their officers. Even those who never see such an academy learn of famous elven battles and heroes. They are celebrated in song and poetry, and dramatized on the stage during holiday festivities. When elves fight, they draw on their long history of both victories and defeats to inform their strategies and tactics. While not all the kindréd make war in the same way, there are some common methods they all share. This chapter provides an overview of elf strategies, battlefield tactics, and naval tactics.

ELF STRATEGIES

Elves have two primary strategic goals that are frequently in conflict with one another. First, elves try to keep their number of war dead to a minimum. Since elves can live for up to 300 years, young elves dying in battle are making a huge sacrifice. The death of a 50 year old human is sad; the death of a 50 year old elf is a tragedy. Only in truly dire situations do elf armies put it all on the line. Generals are willing to temporarily cede territory and lose resources if it means keeping more soldiers alive. Retreating behind the impressive fortifications of cities and fortresses is often the smart play. Towers and walls save lives and it is often better to let the enemy batter themselves bloody than fight a field battle. Last stands and forlorn hopes are sometimes dictated by the grim realities of war, but elf generals always seek other solutions first.

The preciousness of (elf) life has driven advances in medicine and healing that feature prominently in elf eagles. Each talon has at least one and usually three healers as an integrated part of the unit. They are on the battlefield to treat the wounded and save as many as possible. A great aid to this was the invention of an herbal potion known as the Kiss of the

Moon Queen. A swallow of this concoction puts an elf into a trance state that slows down bodily functions. This makes it much less likely that wounded soldiers will bleed to death on the field. Those who survive a battle have an excellent chance of recovery under the care of the master healers. Generals know that ceding the field to adversaries like orcs is a death sentence for the wounded.

The elves' second strategic goal also has its roots in their longevity. Humans (never mind orcs) are often short-sighted. They gratify themselves today and don't think about tomorrow. Elves try to take the long view, and this most certainly applies to the way they make war. When the eagles march, the ensuing battles must be more than a short-term solution. Elf leaders go to war with the goal of permanently ending a threat if at all possible. Sometimes this can be achieved by winning a single overwhelming victory but it is not always that simple. It is often not enough to defeat an invading army. The leadership that drove it to war must be eliminated or its homeland conquered or razed. The important thing for the elves is that they do not have to fight the same enemy every five or ten years.

On first blush, this strategy sounds vicious and it can be. Elven leaders, however, don't look only to military solutions. If they can turn a defeated enemy into a trading partner or an ally, they are happy to do so. Long term alliances with many dwarf city-states and human kingdoms began with wars. Now some enemies – dark lords, orcs, and the like – cannot be made into allies. They must be either defeated totally, or re-directed elsewhere. Bloodying their noses with costly defeats and manipulating them with spycraft can often cause such enemies to seek easier prey or (better yet) fight amongst themselves. These foes are not forgotten about, however. Their activities are watched, and key players are manipulated or pushed into the most foolish and destructive decisions. The end result should be the same: the threat is eliminated.

As you can see, the twin goals of saving elf lives and ending threats permanently are not always going to be harmonious. Generals often must spend lives now to save them in the long term. They do not do this lightly. They know that their dead soldiers are sacrificing their own futures so other elves will have the opportunity to live long, full lives.

BATTLEFIELD TACTICS

While elves are often willing to let their fortifications frustrate attacking enemies, field battles are an almost inevitable part of every war. This is what the eagles train for year after year. When the time for battle comes, units have long practice maneuvering as part of a larger army. Training and discipline are both required to utilize the tactics that follow.

AMBUSH

Pointy ears are running! Follow me over the bridge. There are skulls to crush!
Final words of Dagrud Skullkrusher, Orc Warchief

This is the oldest of all elf battle tactics. It has its roots in the hunting techniques of the early tribes. To kill an animal before it bounds away, a hunter must lure it to the killing ground, surprise it, and strike before it can react. Those same principles apply to the ambush in war. While elves are hardly alone in using ambush tactics, their natural stealth and their skill at archery make them expert practitioners. It's also a tactic that can be used by forces of all size, from the small scouting party to the raiding force to the full blown army. Green elves and moon elves in particular rely on ambushes in warfare, though all the kindred use the tactic.

The first part of a successful ambush is the lure. This is often a unit of troops that seems to be retreating but in reality is leading the enemy where the elves want them to go. Sometimes the terrain itself guides attacking forces to the desired location. Next is the killing field, the place the ambush will be sprung. In many elven lands, good locations are not just chosen in advance but cultivated. Green elves create paths that lead to clearings surrounded by undergrowth, for example, and the secret ways to hidden gold elf

cities are replete with ambush sites. The chosen site must include ample cover for the elves to conceal themselves and little to no cover for the attackers.

When the enemy is fully enmeshed in the trap, a signal is given and the archers let loose. This is a moment of great confusion for the ambushed, as arrows seem to fly from nowhere to kill and wound. It is at this point that the final piece of the puzzle should drop into place. If terrain allows its concealment, a blocking force now moves behind the enemy force. Typically these will be spearmen or swordsmen, backed up with more archers if possible. When enemy troops flee from the ambush site, they run into a wall of formed troops blocking the way. Now hemmed in, foes can be destroyed or taken prisoner unless a successful breakout can be organized. Light cavalry, if available, can run down enemy troops that manage to escape from the ambush.

The green elves' use of the ambush is at its most deadly when they are defending their home forests. In these situations, they do not set up a single ambush, but a whole series of ambushes meant to wear down the invading army's numbers and morale. In addition to the scouts and archers that feature in all elf armies, they have the tree runners, who can rain death down on the enemy from the forest canopy. Fighting in this environment can be an entirely dispiriting experience for the invaders. The green elves may lead enemy troops on for days or even weeks, whittling them away with ambush after ambush until they use their full force to crush the remains of the enemy army entirely.

ARROW STORM

Archers, you have your targets. On my command, loose!
Teralel, Elf Captain

Elf armies contain a higher percentage of missile troops than any other army. Oftentimes, half an army's soldiers will be bowmen, so it only makes sense that archery is at the center of one of the most common of elven tactics. An arrow storm is exactly what it sounds like: volley after volley of arrows crashing down on the enemy battle line. When executed properly, an arrow storm can cripple and break the enemy before the armies even meet blade to blade. It sounds like a simple tactic (shoot lots of arrows; win!) but there is more to it than that.

First, the battlefield must be conducive to archery. The missile units need to be able to see what they are shooting at and the enemy should have little cover to take advantage of. If it is possible to put out ranging stakes before the enemy takes the field, so much the better. Second, the elf force must be well-supplied with arrows. An archer taking aimed shots can empty a quiver in just a few minutes and typically goes into battle with two full quivers. This is enough for a short engagement but for a proper arrow storm more ammunition is needed. The general must ensure it is available. Each talon needs a dedicated wagon parked behind it so a constant supply of fresh arrows can be

provided to the unit. If fighting in defensive works, it's even easier to have stockpiled arrows at hand. Lastly, the units of archers must be deployed appropriately. Generally, that means interspersing units of archers evenly across the battle line, so a good coverage can be achieved. Some battle plans may involve concentrating on certain segments of the enemy line, and then an uneven deployment of units is necessary.

A general using the arrow storm tactic is like a conductor and the army is his orchestra. There will be points in which the best tactic is to have all archer units shooting at the closest enemy targets. Those are the crescendos. In between those there are smaller movements though. A general might open up with only one wing to counter-attacking cavalry, have only the center shoot to encourage the enemy flanks into foolish attacks, or concentrate all shooting on the center of the enemy line. Coordinating these attacks under battlefield conditions is challenging, but elves commonly handle it through signal arrows. The general keeps a talon of archers around him with a variety of signal arrows ready to fire. On his mark the whistling arrows can indicate fresh orders and new targets.

When the general judges that enough damage has been inflicted upon the enemy army, the melee troops can begin their advance. As they move out, the archers maintain their fire, so enemy units will be disrupted when the elves charge home. It takes tremendous discipline on the part of the melee troops to march towards an arrow storm, and true marksmanship on the part of the archers to keep their arrows on target as their own troops get right up on the enemy.

THE DRAGON'S SCALES

When the orc horde came into view, my mouth went dry. Its numbers seemed endless. How could we defeat an army that large? Then I looked behind me and saw thousands of elves ready for the fight. Up the slope were swordsmen and foot knights to support us. On top of the hill were rank upon rank of archers, just waiting for the command to loose. And all around me spearmen, shoulder to shoulder with shields locked. I smiled then, for I knew the dragon's scales would protect me.

Arafel, Elf Spearman

The Dragon's Scales is the standard method of deployment used by high elf eagles and from it several tactics derive. Out in front of the battle lines are skirmishing archers. They are there to neutralize enemy skirmishers and discomfort the enemy's battle line if possible. Behind them the eagle is arrayed in three separate lines. The front line is made up of spearmen in a shield wall formation. Their spears allow them to deal with both cavalry and infantry. Companions, if available, are also placed here in support of the spearmen. The middle line is primarily made up of swordsmen. Their job is to contain and push back any enemy forces that break through the front line. If the eagle contains foot knights, they are often deployed in the center of the middle line and provide the hardest hitting counter-attack. The rear line consists of formed units of archers. Their job is to shoot volleys of arrows over the heads of their comrades to thin out the enemy battle line. Units can also be detached to help neutralize breakthroughs or deal with flank attacks. If the third line can be placed on elevated terrain, so much the better. Anchoring the eagle's flanks are the cavalry. Most generals include a mix of light and heavy cavalry on each wing, though other configurations are possible. Some battles have been fought with heavy cavalry on one flank and light cavalry on the other, or with all the cavalry on one flank because the other is anchored on a river, swamp, or other impassable terrain.

The ensuing formation is a flexible one, able to deal with a variety of enemies and useful on the attack or in defense. When attacking all three lines advance while the light cavalry surges forward to pelt the enemy battle line with arrows in concert with the skirmishers. They may also engage or (even better) lead off enemy cavalry. On the general's command, the rear line stops and its archers begin shooting their volleys. Meanwhile, the first two lines continue forward until they can charge. At this point the heavy cavalry seeks openings on the flanks. If they can drive home a charge while the enemy battle line is already engaged with the infantry, the battle can usually be won. If the heavy cavalry is countered by enemy cavalry or another blocking force, the first two lines must carry the day. Alternatively, the heavy cavalry can be used to make the first charge and punch into the enemy battle line, and then the infantry can follow up and exploit its success.

The Dragon's Scales method is, if anything, even better for defense. Since the archers don't have to move forward, they can begin to shoot as soon as the enemy gets in their effective range. The light cavalry can try to goad rash units into charging ahead of their comrades and exposing themselves to destruction without proper support. The spearmen can set themselves to receive the charge and a ready shield wall is difficult to shift. Heavy cavalry can be used for flanking movements or held back to counter dangerous breakthroughs. If the general knows a defensive battle is to be fought, light ballistas may even be deployed on the flanks for added punch.

THE WYVERN'S STING

What do you mean there's elf cavalry behind us? That is not possible! Have you been into my brandy again?

General Edgerton, (disgraced) Consort of the Iron Queen

The Wyvern's Sting is a common tactic used when eagles have time and room to maneuver. It takes its name from an old saying:

If you only watch the wyvern's maw, it's the sting that will kill you.

It means that you can't become fixated on one thing or you won't see the real danger approaching. The elves refer to the various envelopment tactics they employ as the Wyvern's Sting because they rely on striking where the enemy least expects it.

At its most basic this tactic involves sending a fast moving force on a flank march while the main force keeps the attention of the enemy army fixed upon it. It is important that this flanking force stay away from prying eyes, so setting out at night is common. Special care must be taken to evade or neutralize enemy scouts while on the move. If the flanking force is detected, a canny general will escape the trap or set one of his one. If all goes well, the flanking force can attack the enemy army in its flank or rear once it has engaged the main force. Alternately, it can attack the enemy's camp or supply depots and create havoc in the rear. Trapping an army between two forces after destroying its supplies can lead to a quick victory.

Some generals have had success using more than one flanking force. This is much more difficult to coordinate. Having multiple smaller commands opens them up to being attacked and defeated one by one. Generals that have succeeded in double envelopments have become rightly famous for their victories.

Elf generals have had success with the all-mounted flanking force. This usually consists of light cavalry, heavy cavalry, and dragoons. Such a flying column is very fast indeed and can quickly wrong foot the enemy. All infantry forces can also work if the soldiers are well-trained and take only what they need with them. Campaigns that take place by the water open the possibility of troop movement by ship or boat. Sea elves obviously excel at this type of maneuver and have landed many a flanking force behind enemy lines.

NAVAL TACTICS

Although water travel is not the exclusive province of the sea elves, they are the masters of it. Sea elves maintain large fleets of vessels of all sorts and have used them to explore, trade, and make war throughout the ages. While elves use a dizzying array of boats and ships throughout their realms, when

it comes to naval warfare the sea elves have developed three ships that make up the core of their battle fleets. The lightest ships are known as falcons. They are built for speed and use only sails for propulsion. Falcons are scout ships with small crews. Their job is to find enemy ships, not engage them. The primary fighting ships are called sea serpents. They have two banks of oars and two masts, and usually carry 40 marines and 20 archers, though more can be deployed for some loss of speed. Sea serpents carry one heavy ballista in the prow but their primary method of combat is the boarding action. The heaviest ships are known as dragon turtles. They are large and tall ships, solidly constructed and difficult to sink, with three banks of oars and two masts. They have heavy ballistas fore and aft, and two light ballistas each on the port and starboard sides. Dragon turtles are the slowest elven ships but they are designed to be missile platforms. In addition to their ballistas, they usually have 100 archers on board, and a further 50 marines with long spears to repel boarders. Since they ride high and the marines are experts with their spears, dragon turtles are hard to board.

THE COILS OF THE SERPENT

Archers, I want that deck swept clean. The marines should be able to walk to the hold on a carpet of corpses by the time you are through!

Rafiel, Captain of the Golden Heron

When the goal is to capture enemy ships – for supplies, treasure, intelligence, or just the challenge – sea elves use a tactic called the Coils of the Serpent. Sea serpents typically go hunting in groups of three, sometimes with a falcon to help them find prey. They are fast ships and can overtake most merchant and war ships. Those that can't be caught with speed alone can be maneuvered into a box. Once the sea serpents have their target penned in, two of the ships concentrate on missile fire. They fire their ballistas and shoot arrows at the enemy crew while the third ship closes to board. Sailors throw out grappling hooks and pull the ships together, then the marines board the enemy ship. If the support ships have done their jobs, the marines should have an easy fight. Should things not go as planned, a second sea serpent can come alongside and disgorge its own marines. This is usually enough to finish the job.

In larger engagements, it isn't always possible to employ such favorable odds in boarding actions. If more than a half dozen ships are going to be involved, the sea elves try to bring a dragon turtle with them to provide a heavier weight of fire. This can be tricky, as dragon turtles are slower than sea serpents. If the enemy ships are faster than the dragon turtles, the tactics must change. Sometimes the sea serpents will drive enemy ships into the waiting embrace of the dragon turtles and so trap them. Another option is to use a single dragon turtle as bait, hoping to draw in enemy ships who can't resist such a prize. Once engaged, the enemy ships can be ambushed by the lurking sea serpents.

THE DRAGON'S BREATH

Where's the fleet, your majesty? Burned...all burned...

Xerto, Royal Observer

In times of war there are naval engagements in which the elves' goal is a simple one: destroy the enemy fleet. There is no faster way to do that than fire. When the battle plan is to unleash the Dragon's Breath, the sea serpents and dragon turtles must be prepared. Extra archers need to be deployed to each ship. Barrels of oil or pitch must be loaded to make fire arrows and ballista bolts. Braziers must be brought onto the ships and bolted to the decks to light them. Barrels of sand must also be loaded and fire drills rehearsed. While the plan is to make the enemy fleet burn, a bunch of ships loaded with oil, pitch, and open flames are accidents waiting to happen. All those extra supplies make the ships slower than normal. For this reason a third of the sea serpents sail with their normal equipment and crew. They provide speed and a quick reaction force when necessary.

Once the falcons have spotted the enemy, the elven fleet heads toward it. If the enemy fleet tries to escape, the unladen sea serpents shoot ahead and try to engage it until the rest of the fleet can come up. If the enemy fleet wants to fight, the unladen sea serpents move to the flanks and the rest of the fleet engages. As the two fleets approach, the elves let their fiery missiles fly. The dragon turtles are key to this tactic because they can direct a punishing barrage on any ship in range. While other navies also use war machines and flaming missiles, the real advantage the elves have is their archers. The elven longbow can shoot farther than any other bow or crossbow, so literally thousands of flaming arrows can rain down on the enemy fleet before they can answer in kind. The result is ship after ship going up like oil soaked rags. Those that escape can be hunted down by the falcons and the unladen sea serpents.

THE GRIFFON'S WINGS

*As the Serellian fleet searched for us in vain, we sailed into their harbor and
left their docks and warehouses in ruins.*

Evatal, Captain of the Sea's Embrace

While the Dragon's Breath is a brutal and effective tactic, the fleet that
employs it runs a lot of risks as well. Oftentimes, the sea elves prefer to
achieve their goals by avoiding a big showdown. To do this they use the
speed and maneuverability of their ships to best advantage. When the
decision has been made to use the Griffon's Wings, the dragon turtles stay
in port or are used to defend strategic points. Meanwhile, the rest of the
fleet takes to the sea.

The falcons fan out, scouting out the route the sea serpents plan to take.
Their job is not to bring the fleets together but to keep them apart.
Sometimes this means leading enemy ships away, which can be dangerous
for them. Meanwhile, the sea serpents make for their goal and what this is
can vary. They may raid enemy ports, plunder merchant convoys, sink
unprotected troop ships, or land marines and other troops in support of a
land campaign. Even without facing an enemy fleet, this approach still has
its challenges. There are port defenses, garrisons, unknown nautical
hazards, and other problems to deal with. All the while there is the danger
of the detection and enemy ships coming to attack them when they don't
have the dragon turtles for heavy support.

SIEGE TACTICS

There are many bloody sieges in elven history and although they are
able practitioners, it is not the elves' preferred form of warfare. They leave
such tedium to the dwarves, whose temperament is better suited for it. If
they must be involved in siege warfare, they much prefer to be the
defenders. Elven defenses are cunningly constructed and a small force can
hold out against many times its number. When elves attack, the tactic they
try to avoid is the escalade. Orcs and humans may be eager to throw
themselves onto prepared defenses and die in droves, but to elf generals
this is a last resort. The price is simply too high in all but the most dire of
situations.

If they must take a fortress or city, their preferred method is a surprise
attack. Speed and boldness can often win the day before the threat is even
understood. Such attacks often include sending small advanced forces like
scouts and moon elf infiltrators to find hidden entrances or capture gate

houses. Fast moving forces can then be inside before defenders can even muster, eliminating the need for a siege altogether.

If such a coup de main can't be mounted or does not succeed, then the attacking army will begin digging siege lines and invest the fortress or city. The besieged are then cut off from all aid and left to rot. Sometimes the goal is simply to keep the defenders bottled up while the elf army runs rampant elsewhere. In that case the besiegers only need to be strong enough to keep the cordon tight. If capitulation is necessary and there is time, the elves try to starve the defenders into submission. This can be a long process, and the elves need to be vigilant to breakout attempts from within and relief efforts from without. If the elves have one or more wizards with the army, they may not even need to wait for the defenders to starve. The siege only needs to last long enough for the wizards to cast a suitable ritual. This can be a matter of weeks for a localized effect like a section of wall tumbling down or fouling of wells, or months for more destructive effects like an earthquake or the re-routing of a river to undermine the walls.

ELF VICTORIES

The oldest existing book of elven history, *The Chronicle of Leaf and Stone*, begins with a battle, so war is something all too familiar to the elf kindred. The eons are studded with martial moments of shining glory and tragic heartbreak. A scribe could fill a dozen tomes with tales of elven arms and still there would be more to tell. In this book we must be more selective. It details five battles, one for each of the elf kindred. Each engagement is a famous victory that illustrates the methods and tactics elves use when they go to war.

BATTLE OF THE QUEEN'S EYE

In the depths of an ancient wood is a lake that shines like a mirror in the moonlight. On an island in its center is a stone circle, used for ages in the religious rituals of the elven priesthood. In bygone days green elf clans had roamed the wood but moved on or died out and eventually the only kindred who still came there were the moon elves. On certain nights they could commune with the Moon Queen, and show her that her people honored her still.

For the most part the moon elves had little trouble traveling through the forest to the lake they called the Queen's Eye. One year Valantel, a priestess of the Moon Queen, led her clan to the forest in anticipation of the ritual. Her scouts reported something most troubling: a tribe of gnolls had settled around the lake. Gnolls, fearsome hyena-headed humanoids, were not native to the region. A wizard named Ul'Carnek had brought them here from the north. He was working his own ritual in the stone circle. Valantel didn't know the nature of this ritual but she could not afford to wait and find out. The moon would be full in a matter of days and the Queen's Eye needed to be reclaimed by then.

Valantel conferred with her clan's chief, Meandor. They mustered their warriors and then sent the noncombatants a safe distance away. Their force numbered but a hundred, a mix of swordsmen, archers, scouts, and infiltrators. The gnolls had at least three times as many fighters. Getting them away from the Queen's Eye would not be an easy task.

The following night the moon elves moved into position around the gnoll encampment. The gnolls were not expecting trouble and had only a few sentries posted. The infiltrators took care of them quickly and quietly. Then Valantel led a dozen infiltrators under the docks. When they were in place and ready, an archer fired a signal arrow whose whistle sounded like a forest bird. This was Meandor's signal.

Arrows filled the air and plunged down on the sleeping gnolls. They awoke in confusion, as Meandor's scouts and archers continued to shoot withering volleys. In the camp all was confusion until the gnoll chieftain began to pull his warriors together. Gnoll archers began to fire blindly into the trees while the chieftain got his axemen into a shield wall. This he advanced towards the treeline at a quick pace, even as elven arrows continued to rain down upon them. As the majority of the gnolls moved away from their camp, Valantel and the infiltrators commandeered small boats and began to row to the island.

In the woods the moon elf scouts and archers began to fall back, leading the gnolls away from their camp. The gnolls had their scent now and packs of them split off to pursue small groups of archers. With their quickness and ferocity, the gnolls overwhelmed some of the archers. Other packs were led into waiting units of swordsmen, who ambushed the gnolls and then faded back into the forest. Meandor and his warriors continued to bleed the gnolls until the chieftain had had enough and called the retreat back to camp.

Meanwhile, Valantel and the infiltrators reached the Queen's Eye and made their way to the stone circle. There Ul'Carnek was performing a ritual around a great fire. His bodyguard of 20 gnolls were with him, along with a towering ogre who helped enforce the wizard's will. The gnolls had heard the sounds of battle and were on edge. Quarrels fired from hand crossbows flew out of the darkness. They were small but the moon elves had dipped them in potent venom. Soon the wizard's bodyguards were crashing to the ground and convulsing as the poison tore through their systems. Then the infiltrators were among them with their short, deadly blades.

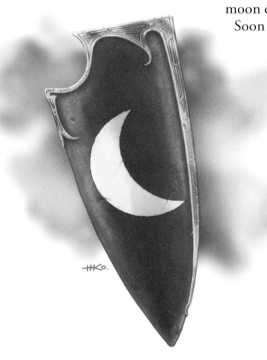

Ul'Carnek was shaken from his mystical trance and saw carnage all about him. He pulled out a wand and fired a blast of ice that froze one infiltrator in his tracks. The ogre smashed another to the ground with his great club. Two more infiltrators engaged the ogre with crescent staves. One kept its attention while the other used her weapon to sever the ogre's tendons. The monster came crashing down and the flashing crescent blades ended its life. Ul'Carnek tried his wand on Valantel but could only stare wide-eyed as she walked through the cloud of ice. "The Moon Queen is my shield!" she shouted, as her blade took Ul'Carnek's head from his shoulders.

When the gnoll chieftain and his warriors returned to the camp they found the heads of Ul'Carnek and his ogre mounted on spears in front of a roaring fire. The survivors fled and did not return. The following night Valantel performed her own ritual and it is said the Moon Queen spoke to her people for the first time in decades. What she said the moon elves will never repeat.

SIEGE OF AVELORN

After he had crushed a human army, the orc warlord Shadderak found himself with a number of prisoners. Most went right into the stewpot but one yammered on in broken orcish that he had a valuable secret. The warlord sent for his shaman to translate and Shadderak interrogated the prisoner. The human, a mercenary named Ruderick, claimed that he knew the location of one of the hidden gold elf cities. Unbelievable plunder could be Shadderak's, but only if he kept Ruderick alive and let him go once he guided to the orcs to the elf city. The orc warlord did like the idea of killing a lot of elves and taking their shiny stuff, so he let Ruderick live. For the time being anyway. He turned the human over to his scouts and told them to lead the horde to the hidden city.

The horde marched for several weeks, eventually approaching a mountain range. As they got closer, units of elven light cavalry began hit and run attacks on the horde. They rode up, unleashed volleys of arrows, and raced away. Shadderak's wolf riders gamely pursued them and always the elves tried to pull them south. Ruderick insisted the correct course was east so the horde kept on its path. It seemed as if only sheer cliff was to their front but this proved an optical illusion. There was a gorge that led into the mountains. The city was that way, claimed Ruderick.

The horde marched up the gorge. Now elf infantry began to attack from above, shooting arrows and dropping stones. A wiser general would have retreated but now Shadderak's blood was up and he kept driving the orcs forward despite casualties. Eventually the gorge widened out into a small valley and there was an elven fortress. It seemed small for a city but Ruderick said that much of the city was underground. This made sense to the orc warlord, so he deployed the horde and began making siege lines.

The fortress was called Avelorn and its commander the battle-tested General Ullator. He had perhaps 500 gold elf soldiers and Shadderak's horde numbered at least 4,000. Ullator sent out messengers for aid before Avelorn was invested and then set about planning his defense with his captains. His greatest advantage was that Avelorn was a training depot for the Knights of the Chalice so fully a third of his troops were heavy infantry. The remainder were spearmen, swordsmen, and archers, and the light cavalry that had tried and failed to redirect the horde. The fortress also had four ballistas mounted on its towers.

Shadderak had brought disassembled war machines with him, and the orcs began to construct the catapults and ballistas. Meanwhile, one of his warchiefs, Krimbaz, loudly proclaimed that he could take the fortress with an immediate assault. Shadderak knew that the warchief was a threat to his position so he ordered the assault and let Krimbaz lead it. The canny

warlord knew an unsupported escalade would fail, so he held back his better troops. The elves filled the attackers with arrows and threw down their ladders. Krimbaz and most of his warband were killed and Shadderak had one problem less. Soon the orc war machines, creaky though they might be, were throwing stones at the fortress. The orcs also readied a large battering ram.

At first Ullator was unconcerned about the orc war machines. They were poorly constructed and inaccurate, and it would take them some time to knock down one of Avelorn's walls or towers. Then a lucky shot hit the front gate and damaged it heavily. This was a worrisome development because Ullator needed time more than anything else. That night Ullator led a sortie out of the fortress with the aim of destroying the war machines. The elves made good progress at first, cutting down many orcs and firing several of the machines. Shadderak responded quickly though and soon the elves had to retreat or get cut off by the orcs' superior numbers.

Ullator had his engineers repair the gate as best they could, and then had them construct barricades in the courtyard beyond. One hundred Knights of the Chalice were quartered nearby. Shadderak meanwhile brooded over his smoldering catapults. The elves hadn't destroyed them all but it would take more time than he wanted to spend to knock down a wall. He had seen what happened to the gate though, and decided that was his way forward. He spent a day re-organizing his horde and then planned an attack for the following day.

That morning the catapults began shooting early. Shadderak ordered them to aim for the gate this time. This proved more difficult than he had predicted, and the horde stood ready all morning and into the afternoon as the catapults missed their target. Finally, as the sun started towards the horizon, a second stone hit the gate and shuddered it. That's what Shadderak had been waiting for. He signaled for an immediate attack.

Orc warbands picked up their siege ladders and moved out. Goblin archers ran ahead and tried to keep the elf archers' heads down. They were only partially successful and soon volleys of arrows were falling on the orcs. Ballista bolts flew from the towers, often skewering two or three orcs at a time. Opposite the gate Shadderak had formed up his Ironbackers, great orcs in plate armor with heavy shields, and they advanced with the battering ram. The warrior infantry got to the wall first and the siege ladders went up. A fierce struggle erupted, as elf spearmen sought to push the ladders off the wall or stab the orcs as they swarmed up. The gold elves were holding the wall but their casualties began to rise. Elf captains called for Ullator to send Knights of the

Chalice to the walls but he refused. He knew where his greatest point of weakness was.

Soon enough there was a great crash at the gate as the Ironbacks slammed their ram home. They had lost a few orcs to archery but their heavy armor and shields let them weather the worst of it. Now the Ironbacks put all their strength into the battering ram. Stones rained down on them from above but still they kept at it. Finally with one last thrust, the orcs knocked the damaged gates in. The Ironbacks roared their war cry and charged into the fortress. Waiting for them in the courtyard were a hundred Knights of the Chalice behind formidable barricades. Now the fight began in earnest. Two units of heavily armored troops locked in a death struggle. The orcs were bigger and stronger but the elves were more skilled and were fighting behind barricades. The contest continued until the sun was setting, swaying back and forth. Finally Ullator and his picked troops charged into the fray and surviving Ironbacks retreated out of the fortress. The courtyard was choked with elf and orc corpses but the gold elves had held.

Shadderak planned to renew the assault in the morning. He had been so close! He received bad news from his wolf riders, however. A large gold elf army had positioned itself outside the gorge, trapping the orcs within. Avelorn had only ever been a border fort. The great gold elf city Ruderick had mistaken it for was hidden much deeper in the mountains. It had sent an army by a different route and now Shadderak was trapped. When the warlord realized his folly, he killed Ruderick and ate his heart. Shadderak and his horde were soon crushed between the fortress and the army. Not one of them escaped to reveal Avelorn's location.

BATTLE OF THE WASTREL PRINCE

King Vlandin of the dwarf City-State of Zhorshun was a vain and paranoid ruler who alienated his own people. He suppressed the guilds and arrested those who tried to re-establish them. He also sought personal glory with a series of ill-advised military ventures. One of the most disastrous of these was King Vlandin's attack on the green elf Kingdom of Thistlewood. The trouble started when the king's son, Prince Zetrosh, visited Thistlewood. Although received and honored by the elf king, Zetrosh got drunk, made several insulting remarks, and then killed one of the king's stags with a repeating crossbow the following day. The prince was lucky he was only escorted to the edge of the forest and told to go home. Nonetheless, King Vlandin declared that the elves had insulted his good name and swore vengeance upon Thistlewood. He mustered his war host and marched to war, despite the protestations of his advisors. He was turning an allied kingdom into an enemy in defense of his wastrel of a son. Vlandin believed he could easily defeat the green elves and burnish his reputation with a conqueror's glory.

King Cadorel of Thistlewood found the whole situation difficult to believe. He sent an envoy to King Vlandin, who first beat up and then cast out the diplomat. An infuriated Cadorel then prepared for war. The dwarves had a long march ahead of them and the country leading to Thistlewood was a flat, open plain. This was perfect country for cavalry – and chariots. Cadorel dispatched his light cavalry and chariots to harass the dwarf war host on its march. They could literally ride circles around the dwarf column, peppering it with arrows and then speeding away. The casualties inflicted were not great but it was demoralizing for the dwarf soldiers to endure these attacks day in and day out. King Cadorel hoped that Vlandin would realize his folly and return home before he got to Thistlewood. Like many foolish men in positions beyond their ability, however, King Vlandin brimmed with confidence. "On to Thistlewood and victory!" he declared.

Once the war host made it to the forest, things only got worse for the dwarves. The gnome allies they expected did not show up (the gnomes being unwilling to sacrifice their own friendship with the green elves). The war wagons were found to be too heavy and ponderous to navigate inside the forest and had to be left on the outskirts. And the very nature of the terrain made it difficult for the dwarf heavy infantry to adopt its usual formation. The captain of the dwarf rangers told King Vlandin it was suicide to go on. The king stripped him of his rank and left him a prisoner with the war wagons (thus inadvertently saving the truth-teller's life).

As the dwarves pushed into the forest, the ambushes began. Skirmisher archers appeared as if from nowhere, poured fire into the dwarves, and then disappeared. Tree runners rained death from above. They found that while dwarf armor could often protect against arrows and javelins, falling stones were much more effective. The green elves then made greater efforts to haul rocks up into the forest canopy for the tree runners' use. Not everything went the elves' way, as the war host still had many skilled officers and veteran soldiers of long service. They found that grenades worked well in the forest and a fusillade from the grenadiers could take a toll from ambushers. Their repeating crossbows also began to take a toll on the tree runners, as they could produce a great volume of fire.

For a week the war host was bled from a thousand cuts and still Vlandin would not admit defeat. When King Cadorel judged the time was right, he maneuvered the war host to one of the great clearings used for chariot races in peaceful times. Here the green elves had arrayed themselves for battle, a shield wall of spearmen in front with ranks of archers behind. Vlandin was ecstatic. Now his heavy infantry could deploy properly. The elves had finally come out and now he would crush them.

The dwarves marched methodically towards the elf shield wall. Arrows arced over the spearmen to crash down upon the dwarves, but their armor and shields gave good protection. Their shields only faced forward, however, and soon the dwarves had a new problem. More elf archers appeared to the flanks of the advancing war host. Then the light cavalry burst from the trees and rode around to their rear. Soon elf arrows were falling on the dwarves from all sides. Great ragged holes appeared in their ranks but still they maintained discipline. At last they neared the elf shieldwall and then they charged.

The long spears of the elves took a toll on the charging dwarves but then the dwarves were in their element. They pushed hard on the elven battle line and it bowed inwards. The more lightly armored green elves could not stand up to dwarf shock troops for very long. The dwarf attack began to slow, however, because the rear of their formations continued to take a beating from nimble horse archers and skirmishing bowmen. The dwarf crossbowmen, out of ammunition, could offer no reply. Finally King Cadorel led his household foot knights in a charge that stopped the dwarf advance cold. First one dwarf unit then another began to beat a fighting retreat. King Vlandin raged against this "treason" but soon had no choice but to join them.

The war host that emerged from Thistlewood was a shattered wreck. King Cadorel let the dwarves retreat. Enough blood had been spilled. King Vlandin survived the disaster only to meet a different fate upon his return home. See Dwarf Warfare for further details.

BATTLE OF YAMANI'S CROSSING

South of the sea elf city-state of Telwing was an expanding human theocracy called Anuritan. Its priests were an unpleasant bunch who burned sacrifices alive to honor their savage god, Vatesh the Flame Bringer. Anuritan had conquered lands to the east, west, and south, but had never moved north. It was a land power and its attempts to challenge Telwing on the sea had all ended in disaster. Furthermore a strait separated the lands of Telwing and Anuritan and this made it difficult for the humans to bring their armies north. Getting their war elephants across the strait was a particularly thorny problem for them.

The sea elves patrolled the strait regularly and generally felt they had little to fear from Anuritan. They did not count on the drive or ingenuity of the priests of Vatesh, however. They pushed their engineers year after year until they came up with a solution to the problem of the strait. They would lash ships together and lay down a road on top of them. This would allow the army and the elephants to march into Telwing. That summer, in what the elves would call bad luck and the humans divine providence, much of Telwing's fleet was sent north to deal with a growing pirate threat. The patrols of the strait thus became infrequent. When the humans began to build their bridge of boats, it went undetected for weeks.

A falcon warship finally spotted what was happening. Human ships tried to stop it but the falcon was too fast and escaped north, carrying the news to the city of Telwing. The commander of the city-state's military, General Faylen, immediately sent light cavalry and dragoons to the crossing site, while preparing the rest of the army to march. She also sent falcons out to find all the nearby warships and order them back to Telwing.

By the time the sea elf cavalry reached the strait, the bridge of boats was almost complete. The dragoons dismounted and began to attack the engineers and crews on the bridge with their bows. The dragoon's numbers were not great, so the humans landed light infantry from small boats of their own. The elf light cavalry, concealed behind a nearby hill, now rode out and caused great mayhem among the landing troops. They shot down many and then rode among them with sabers, driving them back to their own boats. The dragoons and light cavalry kept up these tactics for three days, delaying the completion of the bridge. Finally, the human engineers built mantlets to protect the works crews. It took them a further four days to finish the bridge. As soon as it was ready, the priests sent troops across. The elves harried them with arrows as long as they could and then retreated as the bridgehead was established.

The High Priest of Anuritan, Yamani, came over the bridge with his escort of Templar cavalry. Half his army had made it across the strait and he wanted to be on hand when the elephants crossed. Meanwhile, General Faylen arrived with the main sea elf force. The stage was now set for a battle that would determine the fate of Telwing.

The next morning a sea bird arrived in camp with a message for General Faylen. She smiled and ordered the army to deploy for battle. The sea elf army advanced towards the bridgehead. High Priest Yamani deployed his own troops and sent a message to get the war elephants across immediately. This was easier said than done. It took much coaxing and prodding to get the elephants onto the bridge. By the time the first two were making their way across, the battle had been joined.

Even half the Anuritan army outnumbered that of Telwing, so Yamani was confident of victory. He had heavy cavalry in the form of his Templars and the sea elves had none. When the war elephants made it across, he would complete the destruction of the elves in the name of Vatesh the Flame Bringer. Faylen advanced her battle line. She had spearmen in front backed by companions, with archers on the flanks. Swordsmen, light cavalry, and dragoons were in reserve. Their opponents were mostly medium infantry armed with swords and axes, with supporting crossbowmen and the Templars in reserve.

The sea elves advanced and their archers began to shoot before the crossbows could possibly reply. These volleys hammered the human line, wounding and killing many of the high priest's men. Other commanders would have kept at range as long as possible but Faylen pushed her battle line forward. She wanted to hem the humans in and keep them close to shore. It soon became obvious why that was.

Cries went up on the bridge. Elven ships were bearing down on them. Faylen had only been able to get four of the larger warships here in time, one dragon turtle and three sea serpents. They sailed for the bridge at high speed. Ballistas and then archers fired as they approached, killing troops on the bridge and causing great confusion. The elephants reared and stamped. Then a figure appeared on the prow of the dragon turtle. It was the wizard Adrym. He held his staff high and two bright balls of light flew from its tip towards the bridge. When they struck it, they exploded in fiery splendor. The bridge shuddered as it broke into three

sections, pitching the war elephants and burning men into the water. Soon the whole bridge was engulfed in flame.

Yamani and his force were now trapped in Telwing territory. The two battle lines had come together and were now fighting furiously. The elves were fighting well and his men were dispirited. It was up to the Templars to save the day for Anuritan. He ordered them to flank the elven line and charge. There was only one problem. The Templars had to cross behind the melee before they could move out on the flank, and in doing so they rode by the shore. The elven warships aimed their heavy ballistas and let fly. Their huge spears skewered Templars and horses. Archers on the ships followed up and in a matter of minutes the Templars were annihilated. The sea serpents then beached themselves and marines leaped on the shore. They hit the human battle line from behind and soon the whole thing collapsed. Humans streamed back to the water line and tried to swim for home. Their own small boats rescued some. High Priest Yamani was last seen clinging to a piece of wood while being swept out to sea.

BATTLE OF BLEACHBONE PASS

The Ravillon Empire had once bestridden the continent like a colossus. The high elves had conquered region after region, ever expanding their territory. For centuries the empire remained strong but then cracks began to appear. It lost a territory here, a city-state there. There then followed a span of decades so disastrous they became known as the Dark Century. Towards the end of this period it seemed the final death was on the way. Across the Blackpeak Mountains a new leader had arisen. Her name was Morrikalli, Tyrant of Kheldrassas. She was a dark elf and a demon worshiper like all her traitorous kin. Morrikalli had come to the surface world with a few hundred dark elf warriors and over the course of 30 years had conquered all the land beyond the mountains (for details on one of these battles, see *Orc Warfare*). Ravillon would be next and there was only one way through the Blackpeaks large enough for her army: Bleachbone Pass.

Emperor Taerentin sent out the call across the empire. Although it was smaller than it had once been, he could still assemble a sizeable force. In addition to high elf units from every city, Taerentin's army included gold elf, sea elf, green elf, and Vellador contingents. They rallied in the capital and then marched towards Bleachbone Pass. Everyone knew that the pass took its name from the remains of those who had fought previous battles there. Many understood that their bones were likely to join them.

On their arrival Taerentin's army spent several days skirmishing with Morrikalli's approaching forces. The high elves had gotten there in time to seize the most important piece of terrain inside the pass, a low hill known as Flattop. Some centuries before a high elf commander had ordered the top of the hill removed so he could better deploy his troops there. Taerentin, a keen student of history, had remembered this and brought along ballistas to emplace there. He also stationed archers on the hill and positioned his heavy cavalry out of sight behind it. In front of the hill was the might of the high elf cities. Rank after rank of spearmen, swordsmen, and companions, and in the center of the line the Knights of the Phoenix. On the right flank were the gold elf and Vellador contingents and on the left the green elf and sea elf contingents.

The first of Morrikalli's troops to arrive were orcs. She had two sworn warlords in her service, Krugash and Vaarg. Orcs were fast marchers, so she ordered Krugash ahead with his horde to test the elven line. The orc skirmishers came first, followed by warbands of warrior infantry. They attacked the left flank while the rest of Morrikalli's army deployed behind them. Arrows tore into the orcs, but soon their skirmishers were in range, throwing javelins at the elf lines. Despite great casualties, the orc infantry completed their charge and succeeded in causing some mayhem. The fighting was intense but brief, as the orcs didn't have the numbers. The sea and green elves pushed them back and the orcs retreated. The dead orcs meant nothing to Morrikalli. She was now deployed and she had made her foes spend some resources.

In the center of Morrikalli's line were her dark elf veterans and ogre mercenaries. On her right flank were the two orc hordes and on the left her human contingent, including the heavy cavalry known as the Knights of Kheldrassas. On Morrikalli's signals, braying horns echoed in the pass and her army advanced. The missile troops of both armies began their deadly exchange. Now Emperor Taerentin revealed his first surprise. On the mountains to either side of the pass, the gold elves had long ago excavated hidden galleries and these were now filled with their archers. Now the gold elves plunged arrows into the ranks of the enemy army from above and behind. These wrought a fearful slaughter and caused the wings of Morrikalli's army to pull away from the center to escape it.

Now Morrikalli had her horns sound the charge. Her army had to get to grips with the elven host or they would be shot to pieces. The orcs sped ahead, their berserkers in the lead. In the center dark elf halberdiers and ogre mercenaries charged home, while to their left the human heavy infantry fought their way forward. All across Bleachbone Pass elves, orcs, and men stabbed, bashed, and cut each other in a fearful press. Trouble soon developed on Taerentin's right wing. The Knights of Kheldrassas

charged the Vellador and punched right through them. The gold elves struggled to stem the tide. Taerentin had to release the Griffon Knights, who charged in to save their kin. They smashed the human knights and the line was restored. An orc breakthrough on the left wing similarly had to be reversed by a charge of the Star Knights.

In front of Flattop Hill the battle was at its most brutal. High elves and dark elves met in furious combat. Morrikalli's ogres, their ranks thinned by ballista fire, still took a fearful toll on the high elves. It was the Knights of the Phoenix who finally ended the threat, their great weapons chopping the remaining ogres down. Their move had created a gap in the line, however, and now the dark elf halberdiers charged into it. The high elf archers retreated up the hill and the dark elves surged forward. The archers, however, had retreated to reveal Taerentin's final surprise: moon elves! They had answered the call after all and the disorganized dark elves ran into a perfectly formed phalanx of their hated brethren. The moon elves' wrath was great as they attacked their traitorous kin. They pushed the dark elves down the hill and now infiltrators appeared on their flanks to aid in the slaughter.

Morrikalli could see that her gambit had failed and the center of her line was buckling. She had the horns sound the retreat. Many more fell to missile fire or to the light cavalry that came out to harry them, but enough of her horde survived for her to maintain power. She continued to be a menace for many years but she never again attempted to invade Ravillon. Taerentin used this hard won victory to reverse the decline of the empire and begin a resurgence that seemed unthinkable after the Dark Century.

GLOSSARY

alliance A bond between people, usually to acheive a goal.

ballista A military machine, similar to a crossbow, that was used to throw large missiles.

calamity A state of chaos caused by great misfortune.

cavalry Soldiers on horseback or in some kind of vehicle.

chariot An ancient horse-drawn battle car.

concoction A mixture of various raw ingredients.

glaive A form of broadsword.

halberd An ancient weapon made up of a battle axe on a long pike.

infantry Soldiers trained for hand to hand combat.

longbow A long hand-drawn bow.

pitch An organic material like tar that is used to help start fires. It is highly flammable.

pugnacious Having an argumentative nature.

siege A persistent military attack on a city or other fortified location with the goal of forcing surrender.

skirmish A small battle in war.

FOR MORE INFORMATION

The Arthurian Centre
Slaughterbridge
Camelford, Cornwall PL32 9TT
United Kingdom
Website: http://www.arthur-online.co.uk
Facebook: https://www.facebook.com/The-Arthurian-Centre
 -181341021934874/
Twitter: https://twitter.com/ArthurianCentre
Visitors to the Arthurian Centre can view illustrations, paintings, manuscripts, artifacts, and more that are related to the various legends of King Arthur, the Knights of the Round Table, and Merlin.

The Fantasy Museum
c/o Mist Valley
234 East Market Street, Suite 1
Harrisonburg, VA 22801
(800) 949-5673
Website: http://fantasymuseum.com
Facebook: https://www.facebook.com/theicss
Twitter: https://twitter.com/the_icss
The Fantasy Museum strives to engage the public with the fantasy genre by examining related literature, art, and gaming. Interactive exhibits and games online educate visitors on the history of magic, fantasy, and mythology and acquaint them with the many inhabitants—including wizards—of magical realms.

Institute for Contemporary Shamanic Studies (ICSS)
2106 33 Avenue SW
PO Box 86114 Marda Loop
Calgary, AB T2T 6B7
Canada
(416) 603-4913

Website: http://icss.org

Striving to share shamanic teachings, the ICSS offers classes, seminars, and shamanic guidance and healing. Various programs are open to the public.

International Alchemy Guild

PO Box 22309

Sacramento, CA 95822

Website: http://alchemyguild.memberlodge.org

Facebook: https://www.facebook.com/internationalalchemyguild/

Twitter: https://twitter.com/dwhauck

Members of the Alchemy Guild independently seek to continue the traditions of past alchemists by performing and sharing research and techniques with each other and the public. The guild is also involved in the creation of the first alchemy museum and laboratory in the United States.

Museum of Alchemists and Magicians of Old Prague

Jansky vrsek 8, Prague 1

Czech Republic

Website: http://www.muzeumpovesti.cz/en

Facebook: https://www.facebook.com/mysteriapragensia

Twitter: https://twitter.com/MysteriaPragens

Visitors to the Museum of Alchemists and Magicians of Old Prague can tour the home of Edward Kelley and visit the alchemy lab in which he worked. Texts on display and interactive exhibits allow visitors to better understand the role of alchemy in history and literature.

Science Fiction and Fantasy Writers of America (SFWA)

PO Box 3238

Enfield, CT 06083

Website: http://www.sfwa.org

Facebook: https://www.facebook.com/SFWA.org?fref=ts

Twitter: https://twitter.com/sfwa

SFWA supports writers and readers of the science fiction and fantasy genres. Recommended reading lists, sample lessons, and information for new and experienced writers in the genre are offered on the organization's website.

SF Canada

PO Box 95

Alberta Beach, AB T0E 0A0

Canada

Website: http://northbynotwest.com/sfcanada-wp/
Twitter: https://twitter.com/SFCanadaWriters
SF Canada supports Canadian writers of speculative fiction—fantasy, horror, science fiction, and related genres—by organizing writing groups and meetings and publicizing works by its members.

WEBSITES

Because of the changing nature of internet links, Rosen Publishing has developed an online list of websites related to the subject of this book. This site is updated regularly. Please use this link to access the list:

http://www.rosenlinks.com/CWAR/Elf

FOR FURTHER READING

Allan, Tony. *Civilizations of the World: Exploring the Life, Myth, and Art of the Medieval World*. New York, NY: Rosen Publishing, 2017.

Davies, Owen. *Grimoires: A History of Magic Books*. New York, NY: Oxford University Press, 2010.

Davies, Owen. *Magic: A Very Short Introduction*. New York, NY: Oxford University Press, 2012.

DuQuette, Lon Milo. *Enochian Vision Magick: An Introduction and Practical Guide to the Magick of Dr. John Dee and Edward Kelley*. York Beach, ME: Weiser Books, 2008.

Farrell, Joseph P. *The Philosopher's Stone: Alchemy and the Secret Research for Exotic Matter*. Port Townsend, WA: Feral House, 2009.

Halsall, Guy. *Worlds of Arthur: Facts and Fictions of the Dark Ages*. Oxford, UK: Oxford University Press, 2013.

Hattstein, Markus. *Witness to History: A Visual Chronicle of the World: The Middle Ages and the Early Modern Period*. New York, NY: Rosen Publishing, 2013.

Hauck, Dennis William. *Sorcerer's Stone: A Beginner's Guide to Alchemy*. Sacramento, CA: Crucible Books, 2013.

Hoena, Blake. *Everything Mythology*. Des Moines, IA: National Geographic Children's Books, 2014.

Kelly, Sophia. *What a Beast! A Look-It-Up Guide to the Monsters and Mutants of Mythology* (Mythlopedia). New York, NY: Scholastic, 2010.

Tolkien, J.R.R. *The Fellowship of the Ring*. New York, NY: Allen & Unwin, 1954.

INDEX